"If 'the Christian faith needs a fresh vocabulary and new images to recapture that initial astonishment, to express its radical, world-shattering impact,' then *Between Mirage and Miracle* is a good place to begin to fill that need from the seemingly endless hints of holy connections, perspectives, and even revelations . . . This one you will find to be a good friend with whom you will want to have frequent, enriching conversations."

—JAMES FORBES, Union Theological Seminary

Between Mirage and Miracle

Between Mirage and Miracle

Selected Poems for Seasons, Festivals,
and the Occasional Revelation

J. BARRIE SHEPHERD

WIPF & STOCK · Eugene, Oregon

BETWEEN MIRAGE AND MIRACLE
Selected Poems for Seasons, Festivals, and the Occasional Revelation

Copyright © 2012 J. Barrie Shepherd. All rights reserved. Except for brief quotations in critical publications or reviews, no part of this book may be reproduced in any manner without prior written permission from the publisher. Write: Permissions, Wipf and Stock Publishers, 199 W. 8th Ave., Suite 3, Eugene, OR 97401.

Wipf and Stock
An imprint of Wipf and Stock Publishers
199 W. 8th Ave., Suite 3
Eugene, OR 97401

ISBN 13: 978-1-61097-497-4
Manufactured in the U.S.A.

www.wipfandstock.com
Manufactured in the U.S.A.

*I dedicate this book in gratitude
to the people of Chebeague Island, Maine,
and of the Chebeague United Methodist Church
who, for over forty years, have shared the welcome gifts
of hospitality and community
with true generosity and genuine friendship.*

Book List

Also by J. Barrie Shepherd

Faces by the Wayside
   (Persons Who Encountered Jesus on the Road: A Month
   of Daily Meditations for Advent, Lent, and Other Seasons
   of the Soul)
Whatever Happened to Delight?
   (Preaching the Gospel in Poetry and Parables)
Aspects of Love
   (An Exploration of 1 Corinthians 13)
Faces at the Cross
   (A Lent and Easter Collection of Poetry and Prose)
Faces at the Manger
   (An Advent Christmas Sampler of Poems, Prayers and Meditations)
Seeing with the Soul
   (Daily Meditations on the Parables of Jesus in Luke)
The Moveable Feast
   (Selected Poems for the Christian Year and Beyond)
A Pilgrim's Way
   (Meditations for Lent and Easter)
A Child Is Born
   (Meditations for Advent and Christmas)
Praying the Psalms
   (Daily Meditations on Cherished Psalms)
Prayers from the Mount
   (Daily Meditations on the Sermon on the Mount)
Encounters
   (Poetic Meditations on the Old Testament)
A Diary of Prayer
   (Daily Meditations on the Parables of Jesus)
Diary of Daily Prayer

Contents

Permissions / xi
Preface / xiii

Between Mirage and Miracle / 1
Nunc Dimittis / 2
Forest Snowfall—Before Sunrise / 3
Unseasonable / 4
Ordinary Time / 5
Definition / 6
On Backing Out Over a Sled / 7
Valentine's Day / 8
Trisagion / 9
Ash Wednesday / 10
Looking for Lent / 11
Forecast / 12
Cycle / 13
Septuagesima Sunday / 14
... And Heaven Too? / 15
Peepers / 16
Holy Week /17
Temple Cleansing / 18
Holy Tuesday / 19
Renderings / 20
Rendition (Render unto Caesar . . .) / 22
Mid (Holy) Week / 23
Defining—Holy Thursday / 24
One Kiss / 25
Trade Secrets / 26
Status Report—Saturday / 27

Harrowing / 28
Holy Saturday at the Green Market / 29
First Sunday / 31
Hope Weed / 32
Debriefing / 33
Divine Dilemma? / 34
Two Porpoises Passed By / 35
Wind Sock Kites—Ocean City / 36
Anointings / 37
Real Presence / 38
Lawn Care / 40
Un-dividing Wall / 41
Chesapeake Daybreak / 42
Catch of the Day—Chebeague Island, Maine / 43
Epiphanies Variegated / 44
Alternative Medicine / 45
Hummers / 46
Autumn's Call 47/
Autumn / 48
Terms in Contradiction / 49
Church Picnic / 50
Fall Faith / 51
Digging Dahlias / 52
Daylight Saving / 53
Autumn's Weather / 54
November Dusk—The Eve of Christ the King / 55
Thank Offering / 56
Thanksgiving Wish / 57
Cold Turkey Days / 58
Late Call / 59
Hanging the Greens / 60
Advent Saturday—with Catriona in New York / 61
Aftershave / 62
December Eighteen—Awaiting the First Snowstorm / 63
Revisiting Solstice / 64
Winter Solstice / 65
Pre-Nativity—December 23 / 66
Some Assembly Required / 67

The Coming of the Light / 68
Don't Stop Me / 69
The Silent Seers / 70
The Midwife of Bethlehem / 71
Minimizing Magic / 72
Toltec Point—Winnepesaukee / 73
Seasonings / 74
Bomb Fragment / 75
Dreamhaven / 76
With His Stripes / 77
First Fear / 78
Falling Away / 80
The News So Far . . . / 81
Cadenza—A New Song to the Lord / 82
Stained Glass Windows / 83
Housewarming / 84
Recipe—For a Church Cookbook / 85
Clock Minder / 86
Calling / 87
Eroding / 88
Reasons / 89
Why I Still Go / 90
Significant / 91
Seeing Whole / 92
Secret / 93
Fountain—Brooklyn Botanical Garden / 94
On Hearing Bruckner's Ninth Again / 95
The Beauty of Xiaohe / 96
Amended Credo / 97
A Visit to Saint Paul's Chapel / 98
Mail from New York City / 100
Setting Up the Advent Wreath—November 2001 / 101
Homeland Security—the Eve of Advent / 102
Post Epiphany—January 2002 / 103
Worldly Wisdom? / 104
Lay of the Land / 105

Permissions

Permission to reprint the following poems have been granted.

From *The Christian Century*:
Unseasonable, Ordinary Time, Forecast, Temple Cleansing, Defining, Two Porpoises Passed By, Anointings, Undividing Wall, Epiphanies Variegated, Hummers, Terms in Contradiction, Church Picnic, Thanksgiving Wish, Hanging the Greens, Advent Saturday Morning, Revisiting Solstice, The Coming of the Light, Toltec Point, Bomb Fragment, Dreamhaven, Falling Away, Clock Minder, Significant, Seeing Whole, Post Epiphany

From *Presbyterian Outlook*:
Nunc Dimittis, Cycle, Rendition, Mid Holy Week, Defining, Hope Weed, Debriefing, Lawn Care, Autumn, November Dusk, Thank Offering, Cold Turkey, December 18, Minimizing Magic, Recipe, Stained Glass, Calling, Eroding, Seeing Whole, Amended Credo, A Visit to Saint Paul's Chapel. Looking for Lent, Divine Dilemma?

From *Weavings*:
Trisagion, Septuagesima Sunday, Holy Saturday at the Green Market, Winter Solstice, Silent Seers, The Midwife of Bethlehem, Recipe

From *The New Republic*:
Ash Wednesday, Renderings

From *The Living Church*:
Terms in Contradiction, Forecast, Late Call, The Coming of the Light, Eroding

From *Reflections*:
Temple Cleansing, Renderings, Defining, Holy Saturday at the Green Market, First Sunday, Hope Weed

From *The Cresset*:
Trade Secrets, Lawn Care, Digging Dahlias

From *Praxis*:
Holy Saturday at the Green Market

From *National Catholic Reporter*:
Debriefing

From *The Swarthmorean*:
Terms in Contradiction, Some Assembly Required, The Silent Seers, The Beauty of Xiaohe, Daylight Saving

From *Anglican Theological Review*:
Fountain

From *Perspectives*:
Cold Turkey, Anointings

Preface

SELECTING A VOLUME OF some ninety poems has proved to be more challenging than I had anticipated. It has been over forty years since my first poems were published; and since that date over six hundred of them have appeared in various magazines and other publications, and well over a thousand have been written. A few of them have already appeared in my earlier books. My 2002 Lyman Beecher Lectures at Yale (later published as *Whatever Happened To Delight?*) were liberally illustrated with poetry, much of it my own. *Faces at the Manger* and *Faces at the Cross* also contain a few Christmas and Lenten pieces; while my 1980 self-printed *The Moveable Feast* comprises some seventy of my earliest efforts.

In retrospect, some of my work over the past forty years has seemed to me clumsy and disappointing. Much of it was repetitive, retracing well-worn themes with the seasons of the year and of the church. Several of the poems struck me as rather trite and glib until I remembered they had been written on demand—as it were—to fill in a five or seven line gap in the weekly parish newsletter.

Next came the question of how to arrange the poems I had finally selected. By date of composition, perhaps? Or might I trace continuing themes and topics under which they could be grouped? Finally, realizing that most of them reflected in some way or other the particular seasons, festivals, and holy days of the calendar and the church year, I decided to follow that pattern in the book, tracing the year from January through December, and then adding, at the close, a selection of "timeless" poems that had no specific seasonal reference.

I wrestled with whether or not to provide occasional introductory notes, brief introductions to some of the poems giving, perhaps, the setting and specific spark that triggered the composition. Although this practice is frowned upon today, on the rationale that any good poem should be self-explanatory, I have found, during poetry readings, for example, that such remarks have seemed helpful to the audience. And so I have included them here.

Finally, a word on how to approach this book. Poetry, for me, provides an alternative perspective on reality. So much of our thinking, our communication, our very existing these days is defined by, and confined to, those areas that can be scientifically described and logically proven. Reality, our modern culture insists, consists only of that which can be described, and analyzed in naturalistic and materialistic terms. Yet, while I am a fascinated reader of popular scientific literature, I also find another dimension of my own existence—equally fascinating, equally realistic—which does not lend itself to such analysis, or at the description of which, such analysis fails miserably. Furthermore, this other dimension is composed of elements that make up a major portion of the most important, most vital aspects of my living. These are such elements as beauty and wonder, laughter and tears, the effects of great music, art, and literature, affection, compassion, integrity, and loyalty. It is to this dimension of the indefinable, yet undeniably real, that poetry, or at least my poetry, seeks to speak—not to define it, but perhaps to point toward it, and maybe even describe some of its more enduring characteristics. Flannery O'Connor once wrote that the task of the novelist is not to explain mystery, but to deepen it. I see that also as the challenge that faces the poet.

J. Barrie Shepherd
Wallingford
The Feast of Saint Stephen, 2011

BETWEEN MIRAGE AND MIRACLE

seems to be just where my lines are laid,
that almost-but-not-quite-realm
that proceeds from day to day
without any fresh disturbance
of the regular realities,
yes, your old familiar normality
perceived and then experienced
clear and full, like an old, comfortable shoe,
and, taken all together, not that bad—
quite liveable—considering—
yet still, now and then, shot through,
like semi-liquid silk, with quite another hue
that will surprise and even tantalize
in dreaming, wishing, hoping—
maybe fearing too—when stumbling
into/onto one of those so-very-thin places
where—in delight and even, yes, despair—
an alternate universe slips through
to touch and bless my days
with bright and beckoning uncertainty.

The Nunc Dimittis—Lord, now lettest thou thy servant depart in peace . . . is a traditional prayer of the church, originally uttered by the aged priest Simeon when, after a lifetime of hoping and searching for the Messiah, he is presented in the temple with the infant Jesus.

NUNC DIMITTIS

Well met, bright death!
My search is at its end,
these lingering years of pacing
the tight streets and crooked alleyways,
limping the temple precinct like
a daily beggar, peering,
ever gazing under hoods and shawls
and into faces—"Is it you?"
"Can it be this one?"
"Will the second stranger
that I meet today turn out to be him?"

An awkward peace that was,
that shook the breath from me
as I grasped the squalling child,
a peace that told of turmoil,
swords, tumbled crowns, but also
of a tenderness so terrible
I trembled at the promise of it.
The mother seemed to know
just how I . . . only a girl
yet full of consolation.
Time for sleep.

FOREST SNOWFALL—BEFORE SUNRISE

It is as if the light that is to come
had taken on a flake-like form and substance,
laid itself, in silhouette, along, against,
the windward part
of every naked trunk and branch.
The ground below lies cloaked,
each blade of grass or bracken
with its radiant, glistening garment,
so that, even at the darkest hour last night,
a luminescence shone as if reflected
from whatever burns within,
cast a spell of sheer astonishment,
a silent, clear delight.

Is this, as some have said, only a foretaste
of that truer, fuller, loveliness ahead?
Or might the bright, celestial realm
lie here and now revealed,
its last impediment
my old, reluctant fear to enter in?

UNSEASONABLE

Close to an hour more of light
since December's solstice stood
the calendar on edge, balancing
my dwindling days between the here
and the hereafter.
This late January thaw
has turned thoughts to spring again,
those Holland-ordered bulbs I bedded
late into November already showing
green above the gray and crusted soil.

You'd think, with seventy winters now
beneath my crust, that I'd know better,
learn to stay hunkered warm against those drifts
that still must slump against the garage door.
Yet an old, insistent summoning,
wiser than winter's experts,
sends me back to the seed catalogs,
makes me check trowel, fork and leaf mold,
bends my head to bloom and blossoms yet unseen
but lending never ending fragrance
to every lifeless, frigid scene.

According to the Christian Church calendar the weeks between the various holy seasons and festivals—Lent/Easter, Pentecost, Advent/Christmas/Epiphany—are designated as "Ordinary Time." In effect, most of the year is set within this seemingly pedestrian category.

ORDINARY TIME

These midwinter days that bridge
Epiphany to Lent
can seem anything but ordinary
as the steady waxing light reflects
across old December's glaze of ice,
a biting wind hisses across
the stark bones of the bracken,
and treetops signal sparse
against a sky expecting still
more snow before nightfall.
Scarlet and speckled birds
announce themselves about
the brightness of the holly,
spray from the creek creates
bright frosted chandeliers among
the tangled overhanging branches,
and dusk draws down its spangling
of stars so crystalline they lift the eye—
heart too—toward a principality
that banishes any vestige
of routine predictability.
Ordinariness exists—if at all—
within the desiccated soul,
too distracted by its fearful self
to notice.

Poems can be funny and reflect not only the more sober, even somber, and reflective aspects of life, but also life's undeniably playful and comic side. The next two poems, through both their content and their arrangement on the page, are there for the amusement of the reader.

DEFINITION

S
 n
  o
   w
    is
     for
      stopping
to
         stomping
on
       birdwatching
in
  licking
     off
       looking
          at
slidingoverandunderandthrough
and
   THROWING
at
         people
who
    scowl
        and
curse
    you
        and
      the
      snow.

ON BACKING OUT

Over
a Sled

Funny
  I always wondered
  just how flexible
   you were you tough
                old
                      faded
                              flyer
                                      of
                        the fastest
                    flurried
                flanks
  of far-flung hills.

        Forlorn
       at last
       I find
      the answer.

Nowhere near enough!

The Song of Solomon, with its frankly erotic love poetry, has long been a challenge to pious students of the Scriptures. Thankfully, in recent years, it is increasingly recognized and appreciated simply for what it is: an unabashed celebration of God's gift of sexuality and love.

VALENTINE'S DAY

Dainty
Sainty Day
of scarlet hearts
and pretty pouting posies
when everyone loves everyone
with candy or on cardboard
through the U.S. mail
I'm through with you
and heading back
to sexy Solomon instead
who knew full-blooded bodied joys
of breast and throat and thigh
and sang them cunningly
and wondrous warm
in praise of God
the Maker.

The biblical expression, "Holy, holy, holy . . ." that recurs in praise of God throughout the Scriptures, perhaps most memorably in the call of the prophet Isaiah (Isaiah 6), has also been adopted as a traditional prayer by the Christian church where it is known by its Greek name—
Trisagion or "Thrice Holy."

TRISAGION

A lingering holds my hand
from the switch inside the study door,
leads me instead, caught at the trembling threshold,
to glance across the floor toward the window,
through which there pours a new, uncanny light
to permeate this solitary, predawn hour.
No frost encircled moon or stars are visible above,
yet a definite radiance lights the surface
of last evening's unexpected snowfall,
reveals a scene of branches, twigs and trunks aligned,
outlined against this gentle luminosity.
A fresh discovered world of black and white.
No either-or demanded, nothing to be approved,
deplored, no need to choose, divide the right
from wrong, the damned from the elect.
Rather a surprising, subtle holy, holy, holy—
a glory as of hovering seraphim
that gleams just beneath the skin of everything that is,
and claims and blesses, welcomes me
as part and thankful parcel.

One of my earliest published poems, "Ash Wednesday" originally appeared in The New Republic magazine of February 19, 1972.

ASH WEDNESDAY

Why not
Affirm yourself this Lent,
Be kind and gentle to your you,
Go walking, learn to breathe, read a book,
Know bread and wine and flesh,
Love yourself
Enough to give it
As a gift of love to life,
Or death,
Share hope with one who mourns,
Grief with one who laughs,
And rediscover all the yous
You left behind in getting to this place
From which, with ashes on your head, you go
In search of Easter?

LOOKING FOR LENT

This Lent I'm looking
for a change
no longer giving up
but taking on instead
the task of noticing whatever
has been there unseen
from the beginning
perceiving all those mysteries
monsters too and even
the odd miracle which
until now escaped
my eye caught up
in catching up
who knows
what may be glimpsed
between the lenten rose
and Easter's banks of lilies
perhaps even the footprints
of the gardener himself
whose waking walking word
to us spells seeing
is believing.

FORECAST

Spring did not officially arrive
until two this afternoon,
or so the weatherspinner had informed us,
so that when, at morning prayer,
my still wintered words were interrupted
by a pair of honking calls,
I laughed aloud
to think that my Canadian neighbors
of several springtimes had beaten nature's clock
by seven hours and more to seek
their customary lot along the creek
for hatching this year's brood.

Minutes later—the creed
and half a prayer, no less—
and their first raucous pass to reconnoitre
was followed by the splashdown run,
low now across our deck
and through the clustered trees
onto that quiet pool stretching above the rapids
where, over the next few days, they will be joined,
most likely, by a familiar pair of mallard ducks
who share their taste in shoreline real estate.
Meanwhile a red-tailed hawk
orbits high aloft
in leisurely anticipation.

The computer, with its welcome facility at arranging words on the page, has opened up the way for what are called "Shape Poems." The shape, as I understand it, should express something at least of the content of the poem. I have included a few in this volume.

CYCLE

The more
I see and touch
of birth the more I'm
sure that Spring is all that
life is worth and I and you're
part of the blossoming of
earth and we mature
the more we see
and touch of
birth.

The third Sunday before Lent is called Septuagesima Sunday. The name comes from the Latin word for "seventy" and is derived from counting back seventy days from the Saturday in Holy Week.

SEPTUAGESIMA SUNDAY

Winter dissolves this morning.
The seasoned black on white that lately
meets my weary eye each sunrise
is softened by a mist—drawn after rain—
that blurs all frosted angles,
contours the sharpness of old snowpiles,
and lends a distant gentleness
to those far-off clearings in the woods,
as if some secret blessing lay there
hoping to be explored.

>   Barbara's parting words,
>   written for family and friends,
>   echo from last week's funeral:
>> I've done my work,
>> happy to go,
>> certain of life beyond,
>> reunion . . . and peace eternal.

What little can be seen today,
shrouded by dawn's earliest fog,
unveils a necessary, primeval beauty,
an unsuspected grace within the frigid sleep
transforms mystery to invitation,
dread to momentary silent wonder.

...AND HEAVEN TOO?

Tracing again the time-eroded clauses
of my old, quotidian Credo this spring morning,
I am caught, right at the ritual outset,
by the thought that, given this . . .
this bright expanding splendor
shaped from winter's mud and warming light,
this exuberant rushing green brushing across,
along, the tips, then twigs, then branches,
those splendid-clad mergansers pairing by the creek
and the solemn, blue-gray heron,
given those four—I count them daily—
brand new cottontails, who nibble and then dance
just beyond my study window, springing clear,
for sheer delight, above each other's folded rabbit's ears . . .
given all of this,
this heaven I have learned by rote to also claim
seems quite superfluous, or perhaps lies, tightly curled,
between this dawning moment and the sudden seeing eye.

One of my favorite signs of awakening springtime, after the early emerging of the skunk cabbage, is the shrill calling of the peeper frogs from the swamp, singing for their mates on those earliest warm April evenings.

PEEPERS

"Had my first biopsy today," I murmured,
rejoining the raucous dinner crowd
having peed blood in the spotless powder room.
    No one seemed much surprised,
    and the chat went charging on
    across decaf and dessert
    to gardens, kitchens, children and the war—
        taking, of course, the customary care
        about precisely which opinions
        might be expressed to whom.

On the driveway at departure,
and before ignition keys engaged,
a shrill piping could be heard from the marshes
over by the creek, a springtime urgency of living
that, beneath the fare-thee-wells
and engines' cough and throb, persisted with its fierce,
scarce-heeded, early-April benison.
    And the sainted lady sang
    across the skepticism of the centuries
    that, all things considered,
    all manner of things will still be well.

HOLY WEEK

These weeks between
the ashes and the lilies demand
hardly any getting used to.
The lurking guilt has ever been there,
tight beneath the skin.
While the half-hearted tries
to rectify, those gentle feints toward
righteousness and also loss of weight
seem same-old, same-old, same-old.
But then you find yourself slammed
right up against a cross,
a jagged crown,
torn flesh and blood,
with cries of dereliction.
And who knows what might rise
from all of that?

TEMPLE CLEANSING

Such mad scrambling
    of beggars round the thresholds
        as the shekels flew,
            denarii tumbled in the dust,
    even the sacred temple coinage
            clattered
    to the gutters from the tables of the changers
            overturned in his cold fury.
How the lame then learned to walk,
        even to chase after
             those rolling golden coins,
    the blind picked out the secret glint
            of copper on the cobbles,
    the dumb set up a howling fierce commotion
            over who had grabbed what first!
Surely more healing came about
    through that one swift act of holy anger
        than in three long years of traveling mercies.

Today, again, the beggars
    and the changers ply their trade
        as if the miracles had never come to pass.
Healing,
    like anger,
        can prove to be a passing thing,
            while cleansing never lasts long
                particularly in a temple.

HOLY TUESDAY

Did you drive out money changers
on this day, setting loose the pigeons
and the new-born lambs?
Was today the day the temple-tax fell due
and angler-Peter fished the necessary
from that nearby pond?
Or might this have been the afternoon
you dozed beyond the temple mount,
memorizing the almost-April sunlight,
the sure emerging of the earliest hints of green,
then sat and sipped a flask of Galilean grape—
sweet and slow—on a bench beside a tavern door
and wondered, for the thousandth time,
at what had been and what
was yet to be?

It always struck me as a brilliant move by Jesus to ask his accusers for a coin. In the very act of producing one—a Roman coin bearing Caesar's visage— these holier-than-thou religious leaders demonstrated their disregard for the second commandment which strictly forbade "graven images" of any kind. In effect, they had already sold out to Rome.

RENDERINGS

Is it lawful
to pay taxes? Knifing
trifling terrier snatches at the heels
while the most god-awful murder hatches
crafty in the wheels of smooth despair.
Show me a coin.
Whose image does it wear?
Careful rabbi, never sharing
easy answers, ever further pressing questions
safely not to be examined
even in the private tomb of night.
Yet indictment in this very act
of bearing bony Caesar's visage
or any graven other
in the city holy to the Sinai pact.

Whose image lights
those thirty shiny coins
down in the velvet bag?
Whose copper frown warms
in your palm, deep in the loin,
place you secrete the best from harm,
until the dirty money, proper earned,
returned, can buy a discrete field of blood?
Whose alloy face can occupy
that steep and holiest of holy,
usurp the one majestic image
set when royal we formed man from mud,

pronounced him very good,
and sealed all
with the impress of approval?

Whose image on the coin,
in the palm, the bag,
the heart or groin?
Whose image? Seek it
at the core of him
who laughs with alabaster loves,
lets fly the temple doves,
turns tables toppling and stone tablets,
wines stale water into sparkling,
disrespectfully declines
to purchase death
with life,
and stretching arms for nails
wrenches all from grim Caesar,
and renders all to one.

RENDITION (RENDER UNTO CAESAR . . .)

Unfortunately Caesar's share
has a way of reaching
further than you thought it might,
of catching people unawares so that
they find themselves,
before they know it,
twisting the thumbscrews,
ratcheting the creaking rack,
and pumping at the bellows
to heat the brazier of coals.
Persuaded, nonetheless,
that all they do is
absolutely necessary
in pursuit of evil.

MID (HOLY) WEEK

Was there a weary Wednesday
led into Maundy Thursday?
A day when all that went before—
the palm branches and plotting,
all those traps and snares to nail you down—
or up—the never ending cries for healing,
the stubborn, blind refusal of your fearful friends
to see and speak of what was staring in your face,
all this, and then whatever was to come.
Was this a day when everything came crashing in
until, dashing—mid-dispute—out of the temple court,
you found, at last, a solitary place beyond the wall
to sit and dream, and contemplate tomorrow,
the room, the table, food and wine,
those words that must be spoken,
the lonely walk into the night?

The Thursday before Easter Sunday is traditionally called "Maundy Thursday." The word "Maundy" derives from the Latin "mandatum" meaning "commandment" as I note below. This refers to Jesus' words in John 13:34, "A new commandment I give to you, that you love one another; even as I have loved you . . ."

DEFINING—HOLY THURSDAY

Maundy comes from
<u>mandatum</u>—a commandment
new delivered now by strong
and ready hands, ready to
gird and wash and wipe
both feet and lives
to show us all that
love takes lowliness
to heart and kneels most
readily, an art which also
brings those hands to breaking,
pouring, mending, being pierced
and molding, crafting endlessness
from tombs, grave wrappings,
guards and deadly fear.

ONE KISS

whose brush of flesh
on flesh has lingered almost twenty centuries
should surely have been passion-born,
the fierce and fiery expression of a love
whose sheer intensity burns a bright path
along, across and down the corridors of time.

This kiss, however,
In the flickering torchlight,
deep among the twisted olive trees,
smacked instead of stale betrayal,
the shabby, feigned affection
of one who sought the darkness,
not for deeds of simple tenderness,
but to cover up his shame.
"The one I kiss will be the man.
Take him away and do whatever must be done."

And so the greatest love was ever known
was sold for silver, handed over
in a mockery so vile that kissing,
every gesture of affection, from that night,
has worn the shadowed stain of insincerity,
the mark of dark potential for deceit.

TRADE SECRETS
Things tend to take over.
You might even say he was murdered
by his medium, painter withering on fumes,
carver crushed beneath slip-chain hoisted
block of grinding granite. My grandfather
the tram cleaner died of gangrene
long after one ran over his foot,
or so I was told.
Nails and wood, of course, for him,
turned on him and tore beyond the quick
of his raw carpenter hands and feet.
Getting back, perhaps, after years
of chisel, saw, and adze.
Construction workers know all about it.
That man trapped inside the George
Washington Bridge knows it too well.
When you work too long with something
you get careless, lose the cunning,
then watch out—especially with people.

Theologians have long puzzled over what might have been going on during Holy Saturday while Jesus—God incarnate after all—lay dead in the tomb. The following two poems pose the question and suggest possible answers.

STATUS REPORT—SATURDAY

This time between the times
when time itself hangs in the balances.
This day between two nights when light itself
lies captive to the dark that hunts within.
This moment caught and held between the agony
of ending and the necessity of moving on.
This interval that separates the close of celebration
from the beginning of whatever life can be
stripped of the possibility of sudden laughter.
This concatenation of the cruelest hours
that draws us irresistible as death
toward the birth of still another dawn,
the quickening of a Sunday that will test,
and maybe yet amaze, these fragments that remain
of memory and fractured wonder.

"Harrowing" is an agricultural term for breaking open hard and compacted soil preparatory to sowing the seed. Medieval tradition portrays Jesus as "harrowing Hell" (1 Peter 3:18–20), breaking open the prison house of the damned for the release of captive souls.

HARROWING

So what was going on
that longest day—or almost two—
(Why do they have to call it three?)
between the lifting down and rising up again?

Did he actually crash the ghastly gates of Hell,
fling that wood-and-nail-wrought ransom fee
in Satan's startled face,
and lead a freedom march of the historically damned?

Was he, perhaps, sequestered deep in limbo,
lost in mending prayer and meditation,
maybe even consultation with the Other Two
concerning what came next?

Or did it simply take that length of time
for the Father to persuade his bruised and bloodied boy
to clamber back into the saddle,
considering all that we, and He, had put him through?

The Green Market—Manhattan's first farmers' market in the recent revival of interest in local and organic produce—was located in Union Square, only two blocks from our apartment. My wife and I shopped there Saturday mornings.

HOLY SATURDAY AT THE GREEN MARKET

I think I caught the risen Christ,
just yesterday, on Broadway alongside Union Square.
We were returning from the Green Market
—fresh fish, green mesclun with a pinch
of bright and edible nasturtiums tossed on top,
some tiny new potatoes for our evening meal—
when I glimpsed ahead a shambling, awkward figure
lurching his twisted way along the sidewalk
and jerking fiercely now and then as if in seizure.
He wore a red baseball cap slightly off center,
sweatshirt, jeans, sneakers—all shabby
but well cared for, clean—and over his right arm
a cardboard carton with the lid cut off to shape
a sort of basket, I suppose, to display wares.
I glanced in as we passed and sure enough
there were ball-point pens, other plastic items
in there waiting to be purchased. Silent—
in my head—I wondered at the courage of one
so violently deformed, yet coping, contriving
to survive this predatory city.

Those contorted legs could not move him
that fast and we were swiftly past him to confront,
lying across a heap of trash bags up against the wall,
a homeless man, asleep, with the usual pathetic sign
informing all and sundry:
        I'm in trouble, please help. Someday
        I may be able to do the same for you.

I walked on, ignored both plea and promise,
passed right by as I've been taught to
by this casual, careless, care-less cruel city;
then glancing back over my shoulder saw our friend
in the red baseball cap struggle across,
laboriously read—how long it seemed to take—
that grubby and ill-lettered sign, then lean
over and drop something in the cup.

Yes, I realize, it only encourages. I know
they'll likely spend it all on booze. I've heard
and lived these arguments, knowing far too much,
believing far too little, and being so afraid,
for years now. But there was something in
that simple act, an eastered innocence
put me to shame, drove me to my knees
among the sidewalk lily vendors.
I think I caught the risen Christ,
a day early, but there just the same,
on Broadway yesterday alongside Union Square.

After almost two thousand years the Easter Gospel—Christ is risen! He is risen indeed!—has become so familiar in our culture as to be almost a cliché. It tends to be seen as old news, rather than good news. The Christian faith needs a fresh vocabulary, new images to recapture that initial astonishment, to express its radical, world-shattering impact.

FIRST SUNDAY

And was that a rising like bread, or like mountains,
Explosive like ball over fence, bloom in Spring,
Or steady, relentless, as waves in the ocean,
Or steeples on churches, or gull's soaring wing?

Or perhaps it was human, like waking in April
With sun on your face, and a foretaste so wild,
And a spring in your marrow no winter can frost-kill,
And the light lifting lilt in the eyes of a child,
And the lilt in the eyes of a child.

One of my most published, and requested poems, "Hope Weed" describes an Easter Sunday afternoon when, after an exhausting morning and a refreshing nap, I decided to tackle some problems in the manse garden.

HOPE WEED

Our Christian symbols seem, at times, not quite
appropriate to the meaning that they bear.
For instance, take the Easter lily, white
and fragile sign of resurrection. Rare,
its graceful silent trumpet greets the light
of March or April only under glare
of florists' lamps, unnaturally bright.
You never find them in the open air
before July. A better flower for Easter Day
would be, as every angry gardener knows,
the dandelion, seeded by the gay
abandoned wind that, as it listeth, blows.
No matter how we weed out every stray,
digging as deep, the root still deeper goes.
And when, at last, we quit and go away
the rain falls, and a host of fresh bright foes
stands resurrected, and the garden glows.

DEBRIEFING

So I showed them things.
Not much that was spectacular,
more the usual, ordinary stuff
like wild flowers, birds and seeds,
the daily chores, you know,
sweeping, baking, planting,
fishing, getting along.
I simply pointed them
to what was always out there
and then told them to "Go figure..."
I guess they did,
or did their best at least,
because they kept on coming back
for more, more of them too,
until the crowds began to draw
attention, began to look, to some,
like mobs, began to worry those
who worry about such scenes.
It didn't take them long—never does—
to detect some kind of threat,
something to be got rid of
before it got too late.
The rest, of course, is history.
Or was.

DIVINE DILEMMA?

Well, yes,
I told them I was there
for the sake of everyone and everything.
But they kept insisting, "Excepting him . . . or her,
of course, and surely not for these or those."
I displayed, portrayed, lived out for them
the breadth of your divine embrace
as being universal, reaching, touching each
and all, whenever, wherever and whatever.
But all they could add was, "Only if . . ."
"Hardly this . . ." and "What about . . . ?"
In the end I did it anyway,
spoke, at the last, of your forgiveness
even for the ones who carried out
the spitting, flogging and those nails.
Do you believe they'll ever work it out?
Or will we have to build a Hell
just to make them glad to be here?

During the week following Easter pastors often attend conferences or retreats, in part to recuperate from the pressures of Lent and Holy Week. The next two poems were written at a clergy conference on dealing with stress, held at the shore in Ocean City, Maryland.

TWO PORPOISES PASSED BY

A pair they made
darkly-matched angled
fins lunging among, across
the blue and sparkling ocean
spread beyond the boardwalk
past the panoramic windows of
our pastors' conference hotel.

We were praying at
the time, striving—closed-eyed—
to lose our stress, find
souls again, and all
in thirty hours or less, before
the plunging back into the daily
mess and management.

My eyes were slitted-open,
unwilling to relinquish that
bright tantalizing scene below,
balm to my sight,
worn down by paper scanning,
the cursor's light green
tracing on the screen.

And so I caught the deep
and dreadful brushing-by of mystery,
exulted, silent, in the moving,
living presence of an alien world
that swept along our shores, just as
it does, and is, in each and every
moment, whether we watch or pray
or wake or sleep.

WIND SOCK KITES
OCEAN CITY

They whirled in madly-striped delight
        two swirling catchers of the wind
            tethered like leaping fish on giant rods
                with wild gesticulating tails that played
                    their motions out toward the sea-and-sky
                            horizon and beyond . . .
                    —Something about their structure
        —skilful sewn around the lip—made them
    turn and turn about themselves buffeting
  in a splendid onshore breeze: filled with
nothing—no thing there—yet consecrating
    every thing and every where.

Tibetan prayer wheels
    along the Jersey shore
        flinging forth and naming
                full and round
        an unseen power that sweeps
    and sings—beyond all sound
—the glory of our days.

ANOINTINGS

Those tongues that thronged
on Pentecost have never ceased,
have hardly taken time to swallow,
draw one gasping breath since then.
They sound forth in each and every throbbing
wavelength gathered in by human ears even,
probably, by dogs and bats, persuading,
ever persuading one and all to be
persuaded they are absolutely right.
But that bright descending fire
that melted hearts to kindness sent them
out across all gulfs to spend themselves for
others' sakes, what put it out? Or why has it
flamed fainter, ever fainter with the years?
Is there a sacred oil can yet rekindle such a spark?
Or are we doomed to batter one another with
the truth through the encroaching dark?

New York's annual Gay Pride Parade, usually held on a hot June Sunday afternoon, marched down Fifth Avenue and ended just past the church I served. First Presbyterian set up water tables outside the church doors to serve thirsty marchers with "a cup of cold water in Christ's name."

REAL PRESENCE

Yes, a frilly pink tutu
was, more or less—
more less than more—all he wore,
that and a pair of teetering
stiletto heels and parasol, from tip
to toe in matching lurid pink,
strutting from side to side
his jet-glow black and body-built stuff
in flagrant full gay pride
parading down Fifth Avenue.

From giant urns outside our church
we plied the marching throng
with plastic cups "o' kindness yet"
on a hot June afternoon—"in Jesus' Name."
Fully clothed, and more—
dark clergy suit, black shirt and
stiff white collar—I stood my ground,
clutching a tray of cooling draughts
to represent a welcome and a blessing—
at the least—as child of God.

Beaming, he tripped across,
bestowing smiles—spectacular—on all
and sundry; chiefly me. Daintily he took
the cup I offered, leaned perilous close—
those tipping heels!—and kissed me on
one startled cheek, his rough bristled lips—
generous smile notwithstanding—brushing

deep, appalled revulsion through my gut,
despite all my head was murmuring
of tolerance and Christian love.

"Oh Reverend," laughed the lady
from the sewing circle,
"you should see the juicy kiss mark
on your cheek." And as we both dissolved
in honest, healing laughter,
first head, then heart took over
from my gut and raised a prayer
of thanks for grace's all-too-often
way of shoving me, still screaming,
toward birth.

LAWN CARE

This ever springing green defies us
tricks us with her wiles and tries us
hides her earthy smiles at toil and sweat
secret grows with any slightest touch
of wet or brightness to her skin
bides her easy time until that day
she throws her final heavy blanket
over all our eager efforts.
"All flesh is grass," we say
praying the reaper's blade
will lightly pass across our turf.

UN-DIVIDING WALL

It curves in rugged Pennsylvania stone
a cusp, new moon, above the grassy circle
at the center of the church Memorial Garden
a wall dividing life from solid, stony death.
Five feet tall of it, with flagstone brim
and seven plates of bronze to wear
the names and dates which represent
too much for any wall to bear.
Today's picnic for the Sunday School
has spilled across the lawns into this space
preserved for memories and ashes—dust to dust.
Huddled in sycamore shade and sipping punch,
parents watch with mixed response—some anxious,
others smiling, some seem shocked—as eight
and nine and ten year-olds—defying death—
struggle to scramble up its rough-hewn face,
dance a moment of delight along the parapet,
then dare to leap down to the green below as if
some year-worn craggy granddaddy had beckoned
them to his lap and sat there chuckling
at their wriggling pranks, their shrieks
and whoops and giggles of pure joy. Walls are
for climbing too, I realized, and launching
off the top into tomorrow seeking flight
from memory into hope, then landing
with a thud where tears are swept away
by peals of lively ever-youthful laughter.

CHESAPEAKE DAYBREAK

It dawns on me,
despite the blanket's
warm and welcome weight, that these birds
have decided I shall not miss this moment,
their waking calls crescending now into
whatever mending fantasies flowed
through my sleeping soul.
Beyond the wide-cranked window
an iridescent band divides the sky—
already bright—from the still shadowed
land below. The water of the bay,
bare-ruffled by new stirring breeze,
acts as mediator, sharing the dark,
metallic tones, yet yielding near the edges
to a dancing, deep-reflected lustre.
While the disk itself,
surprising by its rapid rise
from slimmest cusp to ripe, full-breasted orb,
amazes once again by the way it still can jolt
the heart after so many such occasions.
Descending to the broad verandah,
I am halted by the sweeping fragrance of mid-June,
a mix of rose with rhododendron, laurel too, so that,
groping toward a wicker-white and easy rocker,
I feel sated, rediscovering the relentless,
brimming generosity of how each day begins.

CATCH OF THE DAY—CHEBEAGUE ISLAND, MAINE

Their throbbing diesels moving past the point,
and then the whispering wash
of wake breaking along the shingle,
shape a steady counter melody—cantus firmus—
to my time-worn litany of dawn devotion—
psalm, creed and collect, lectionary,
and that listing of the names
to call forth lives beset, or just set down
for daily murmuring toward the light.

And all the while, behind,
beyond this daybreak's earliest birdsongs,
the lobster boats head out toward Broad Sound
and then the open bay, cutting in close here
where we live on the East End,
to avoid the unseen menace of the ledge
that, earlier this spring, as so often in past years,
cost one of them a new propeller, rudder,
a couple cans of bottom paint.

Their dream, as mine—
afloat upon a steep and surging mystery—
to lure and catch a portion of life's bounty,
a momentary savoring, at least,
of an elusive sweetness that lies hidden
in the old, encircling deep.

One of my favorite activities at our island summer home off the Maine coast is berry picking—blueberries, blackberries and raspberries. I share this delight with my three granddaughters and have recently taken up making jam and jelly from the results of our harvesting.

EPIPHANIES VARIEGATED

Every bush may be ablaze with God
as Elizabeth Barrett claimed so famously,
but not every bush is also blessed,
along its bending branches,
by glossy, plump and August-ripened blackberries.
The poet didn't have much good to say for berry picking,
flat-out accusing most of us of sitting
round that burning Bush and helping ourselves
to sweet, seductive fruit, oblivious
to the incandescent miracle.
But the Book itself said nothing about berries.
And if there had been brambles—
I mean out in the wilderness like that—
they surely would have seemed, suspended there,
so downright sacred, ripe to bursting
with the purple, sour-sweet tang of summer's heat
and rain and sunlight, I'd be prepared to lay a bet
that even stammering, shoeless Moses would reach out
at least one eager hand—finger and thumb—
to gather in a palm cup full, then cram them
eagerly between his desert-dry, parched lips,
and wonder at the ripeness to be found
in life that darkens, through a daily, earthy glory,
to a fullness feeds a multitude of hungers,
yet, for all that, never is consumed.
O taste and see . . .

ALTERNATIVE MEDICINE

Took ten minutes to go berrying this morning
looking for healing from the constant wear
and tear—tears too—of being who
I make myself to be most of these years.
But the pickings were so sparse,
legacy of one harsh winter
and late spring that saw
the roof of my tin shed collapse
beneath the frigid mass—
twenty-one inches so they tell—
the mackerel return to our bay
almost one whole month behind,
pickings were so rare all I could find
among the barely forming clusters
there beside the path were three
(almost) ripe blackberries, then bending
close to earth one tiny, grey-black blueberry
no bigger than a dewdrop.
Got pricked for my pains too,
or for my pleasures maybe, since
one of the three already bore that
mending tart and midnight sweetness brings
back, even in such thrifty taste, the benison
of August woods and islands salt with
bayberry and myrtle, cry of gulls,
the silent shoreline presence
of the whales.

HUMMERS

Even in Maine's rain and fog I catch them,
often in pairs, or waiting, patient, perched on
a scarcely bending twig of our aged forsythia,
then working the window box petunias
till the coast seems clear, while I hover, motionless,
on the shadowed porch, hungry for still another glimpse
of ruby throat and emerald layered coat,
the delicate dip of beak in cup, the tilted head,
the blur of wings, that sudden flash of movement—
now-you-see-me-now-you-don't.
Whatever it may be in me—
some wandered/wondered child—
that makes me watch and wait, this late,
the daily hours to catch their, almost holy, visitations,
I'm grateful for it, mindful too
of one who every once in a long while, still hovers
back there just beyond, behind the nearest edge
of solitude, or prayer, or even glimpses
of the tiniest of birds.

AUTUMN'S CALL

The year falls into place
around this season.
Spring's inexhaustible exhilaration
looks a mite less new, not quite
unprecedented, viewed across
the open-oven days of August.
While March's dreary waiting for
the earliest touch of green
seems plain ridiculous when seen along
these bold and vivid avenues.
Yet gold begins to fall just as it forms.
And glory starts to shed itself even
before the robe is fully donned.
Now harvest sounds its mellow, winding horn.
While we stretch tall as corn
before the reaper.

AUTUMN

These falling dawns
and days descend toward
the fullness of the winter fireside,
all those festivals, familiar feasts
by means of which we hold at bay
the coldness and the dark,
portray an inner harvesting
which garners tenderness,
fond memory and song
within the chambered storehouse
of the mind to light with liquid
melody the long and lingering
latterness of life.

Part of the fun in poetry for me is simply playing with words, using the same words with different contexts or meanings, setting them together in surprising ways. This poem is one example.

TERMS IN CONTRADICTION

Leaves are to be left,
I should have thought, to form
a winter carpet for the ground,
a layered blanket snug around
the roots of shrubs and bushes,
ornamental trees, prevent the frost
from pushing in its fatal fingers.
Leaving, indeed, is just what they
cry out for, as they scrape and scuttle,
free at last, along the path, progress
in fits and starts across the lawn and end up
tangled in the long-abandoned flower beds.
Why, then, this energetic, back-and-
shoulder-testing tidiness that insists
on raking, heaping, organizing into piles
or plastic bags to be disposed of by the
authorized collectors? Why this rush
to brush away the last mementos of the
summer's welcome shade, Fall's golden glory?
Oh yes, the neighbors might complain; and when
the rain comes they do mat into a mass
that chokes the precious grass below.
I'd leave them, just the same; obey
the clear, inviting implication of that name,
and find an easier way—a poem perhaps—
to claim my place within the turning of the year.

One late autumn day a bunch of jaded urbanites flee Manhattan by chartered bus for a woodland camp on the far outer fringes of the city.

CHURCH PICNIC

A dozen geese exploding into flight
their wings blurring the autumn foliage
as they pass against the farther shore,
into the light that filters long
across the leaf-strewn surface of the lake.
Nothing better to do but sit and lift
city white faces to the late-departing sun,
lend an ear, from time to time,
to a new neighbor on the wooden bench,
contemplate apples, pumpkins, babies and
mortality, not necessarily in
that particular order,
oversee a sunlit game of bridge
for no stakes visible, small talk of music,
old times, absent friends, baseball and recipes,
the driver napping in a nearby tree house,
until the bus heads southward into night,
tracing the lingering ways of sun and geese,
bearing its harvest crop—surprising peace
toward the dusk that murmurs
news of winter.

Jesus' parables seem filled with harvests, seeds and growing things. The next two poems also seek to disclose the kingdom of God, and the gestures of faith, right at the heart of everyday reality.

FALL FAITH

Today we combed the flower beds for Spring,
A father and two scavenging little girls,
Feeling among the fertile deaths of Fall
For next year's garden. Labeling our crop
Of gleanings into Fiona's extra
Birth Announcement envelopes.
P for Petunia, N for Nasturtium,
I—Impatiens, S—Snapdragon.
"See, this one has an ant in its mouth."
Small harvest heaps we built
Pods, motes, and corms, and curls,
Time capsules, May through August gaiety,
Granaried against another, unseen sun.

Thus faith, we pass it on from day to day.
Not listing, systematic presentation,
No catechismic, roting recitation
Of the "I believes."
A cellar work bench piled
With Fiona's extra Birth Announcement envelopes,
P for Petunia, I—Impatiens,
S—Snapdragon . . .
Tokens, earnests, pledges sealed,
Outward and visible signs
of inward and spiritual hope,
Of warmth, of growth, of gaiety,
And of glory.

DIGGING DAHLIAS

Blackened
by the first snap
of this early winter
dry leaves crisp into powder
as I grasp the chill green stems
still juicy from fall's long blossoming
star bursts and suns of alternating color.
The spade is stamped blade deep
into the steep surrounding soil,
then, wedge-like, pressed back
till the surface cracks wide open
setting free the frost-tipped fingers.
Such a plump and grasping hand
has gathered over summer, clasping,
squeezing vibrant life out of the loamy earth!
Now box them home
and store them careful,
since you know their hidden worth,
basement cool, fox dry, and dark awhile
until some April weekend you can try
uncovering, then smile to see
the pink and sprouting signs
of secret universes
yet to be.

DAYLIGHT SAVING

Brief, busy, and disorienting season,
arriving unexpected, almost, twice each year,
when digits blink alarm at you from coffee-maker,
car and VCR, until your digits are deployed
in seeking, pressing, turning tiny buttons.
A tedious day or two, at least,
of patient synchronizing—There's another we forgot!—
and when the shifting's done,
whatever's gained or lost, the actual moments
stay the same, only the names must change
to protect the innocent.

"Spring forward—" people say,
"Fall back . . ." not only to remind which way to turn,
but to sustain that steep illusion of control,
as if we had the power to move around, adjust,
far less to add or take away, the merest instant
of this mystery we measure ourselves by.
As for saving time; that turning rests beyond,
beneath, above, all springs and falls, whenever—
choice or chance—we can ignore, forget,
escape the calibrating clock, and find
ourselves born—blinking—into now.

Grief and loss increasingly accompany our days as we grow older. However the autumn season, somehow, seems to make such absences even more poignant, more difficult to bear.

AUTUMN'S WEATHER

David's service was last Saturday,
Paul's, back home in Scotland, just the week before.
Mary's depression finally won out
a couple of months ago, while Penny, Bill too,
missed all of summer, leaving us last spring.
Andrew beat the lot, departing for the distant shore
three years ago and more—spoke to his widow
just the other day. While Anne, Joe too,
both recently received the grim oncologist's
penultimate prognosis.

They come in an unholy rush,
these random, brutal losings, rough tearing
at the circle of the years, leaving jagged gaps
that never will, or can, or even should be filled,
erasing—name and place by place—
the time-worn pages of my tattered old address book,
reminding me again, and yet again, how late it is,
how much has been, how little left to be,
how cherished, and how vulnerable
this life-long bond which bears me
grieving on toward another closing of the year.

One of the burdens—and blessings?—of the preacher's calling is the challenge to "climb the pulpit stairs" Sunday after Sunday, regardless of one's momentary mental, emotional or spiritual status, and proclaim the eternal good news of the gospel.

NOVEMBER DUSK—THE EVE OF CHRIST THE KING

Gray, fading, year-worn light
portends an absence of anticipation.
No consideration, even, as to whether
or not it will begin again after
the evident onset of the dark.
A sterile, non-expectant hush enfolds
the city streets below related, I assume.
to the most-travelled-holiday-of-the-year.

Awakening from brief but burdened sleep,
unwilling to resume these shallow interests
that mask decline and fall, I permit
the full weight of the ordinary to occupy
my consciousness, remembering as far back
as I can—as child, young man, new father—
other wakenings into this wintered sense
of raw futility, the clear lack of any motive
to do anything, or nothing.

Tomorrow I must climb the pulpit stairs
and—quaking—sing of royalty and reason,
of a late-November life and death that,
seasoned by sheer majesty, could glimpse,
bestow the pain-embracing promise
of an April sunrise far beyond
the treason of these waking moments,
shadowing hours and days.

THANK OFFERING

Gratitude, if and when it does arrive,
seems very seldom centred on the meal itself.
Yes, the sacred bird with all its panoply
is blessed in solemn, if embarassed grace.
But these days we find it difficult
to face a feast with easy stomachs.
Guilt, that queasy, well-fed luxury,
has robbed us of the revelry of banqueting
while others waste from hunger.

Thanks do break in, however,
here and there, beyond the groaning board,
for bare trees to wander through, a daring child
to wonder "Why?" for one spare day to taste
the last sharp apple-tang of Fall,
gleaning ripe memories of a twelve month passing,
or of other days like this one, other years,
when life rose tall in reverie, death seemed almost mellow,
for a crisp foretaste of the dark and ice that wait,
spiced with a secret confidence that fire will warm
and light us yet into another Spring that hopes eternal,
for an essential rightness, which breathes—
despite the headlines and the daily hurt—
through every pore of this rare day and names it
bright and good, and claims the whole,
in every worn and broken part, for God . . .
such are the thanks we murmur to the living air.

THANKSGIVING WISH

For thanks I'd like to share
a broken line or two of verse,
soup and a sandwich,
maybe a movie, or a fierce
log fire, a winter-seeking walk
among tall forest firs,
salted breezes from the sea,
a chickadee sonata, tiny, terse,
all this, or any part
to lift the rich oppressive curse
that fills this holy day with fatness.

COLD TURKEY DAYS

For those who can deny the malls,
and flying footballs on the screen,
there lies, tucked in between the feasting
and those first December days,
a blessed intermission, several hours,
at least, when nothing must be done,
perhaps a little clean-up time,
the daily paper to be read, for once,
from front to back, a walk through woods
or city streets, no matter where,
don't hurry, find a way to see,
a fire to build with branches, log
and flame, then fall asleep beside,
a child—yours or your child's child—
to forget time with in play that is
as old as time itself. These,
and a wealth of easy open moments,
wait within the unclaimed hours
of these rarely gifted,
all but holy days.

LATE CALL

What do the geese cry
  one to another, angling
    across the early winter sky
      this Advent morning? Surely
        it is a call of courage, of
          encouragement passing by, the
            cheering hope, keen expectation
              of neglectful fields, smooth waters
                up ahead before the darkness settles in.
              Today I waited for them knowing high
            within the bones—far from my brain
            but somehow surer—they would wing
          along and lift and carry me to spy
        the bright, full world that waits
      beyond the vee, prepares to greet
    our landing, honking, jostling
shrill arrival. Oh, take me!

HANGING THE GREENS

We bring the outside in
this chill and waning season,
cut boughs and branches, strands
of light and living green and deck
them all about the walls and ledges
of our houses, make believe we fashion
an enchanted forest glade to frame
our festive celebrations.
Evergreens, we call them,
though they bleed and die,
so soon, in overheated rooms.
Yet that dying lends a fragrance
and a grace, foretells, if we
will heed, another time and space,
where tree and thorns, no longer green,
fulfil their cruel, necessary function
in the bright evergreening
of our wintered race.

A pre-Christmas family weekend in New York City years ago led to a grace-filled moment as the mystery of incarnation is glimpsed through music and the tender hurt and hope of parenthood.

ADVENT SATURDAY—WITH CATRIONA IN NEW YORK

Hanging on beside you as the crosstown bus
lurches its laden way between the wintered hills
of Central Park, my sidelong glance snags
on a prospect never caught before,
glimpsing within your early teenage profile
the full maturity of middle age, the aspect you
will wear one day as mother, matron,
one who bears the future on firm shoulders.
But see now what the eyes betray
in that slightest hint of drawing down toward the edge,
as though a weariness lies buried,
waiting to be born.
My own well-worn paternal eyes seek momentary refuge;
only to be captured, upon opening,
by the clear, unclouded sunrise of your smile.
Thanking the great Provider of such moments
over thirteen years of grace, I leave the crowded bus,
lead you dashing across Madison, into elegant Saint James'
to meet, beneath the Advent wreath, a harpsichord
and string ensemble, rehearsing with the soloists
tomorrow's version of Messiah.
> Behold a virgin shall conceive,
> And bear a son,
> And shall call his name,
> Immanuel—God with us.

And through a sudden storm of tears
I grasp the wounding, mending holly branch,
claiming the spiral mystery of word made flesh
and secret lodged within the solemn
turning of the years.

*Another pre-Christmas New York scene;
this time at the revolving doors to Macys.*

AFTERSHAVE

Try a little Eternity,
he murmured, gently spritzing me
as I powered through the miracle
on 34th street doors of Macy's,
intent on finding one last thing
to make my Christmas list complete.
Try a little Eternity.
And stopped me short, mid headlong dash,
to say, Why not? A splash of aftershave—
Quelle est cette odeur agreable?—
might even bring a fragment (figment?)
Of that frankincensing cowshed
to bless my frantic quest with,
at least, momentary mystery,
a fragrance sorely wanting
in this flagrant race to beat the 25th.
Who knows but, at that higher,
heavenlier turnstile, the old geezer
perched behind the book might just lean
across his podium with a holy spraygun
of his own and, spritzing madly, murmur,
Here Barrie, now try a little Eternity.

DECEMBER EIGHTEEN—
AWAITING THE FIRST SNOWSTORM

Three to five inches,
that's what they're saying,
overnight into the morning hours.
And taillights glow as streets and parking lots,
supermarkets too, throng with over-prudent seekers
preparing for disaster yet again,
secret hoping that perhaps this time
they will actually get to use those candles,
cans of Campbells, and the pack
of extra batteries.

Home, I lower blinds against the dark,
sensing a gathering in the air,
a suspended, swaddling silence
pregnant with a multitude shimmering flakes,
ready, despite the accumulated evidence
of seventy-four past winters,
to be surprised once more—
surprised almost to kneeling in the gentle stuff—
at what this ordinary, too familiar world
can do with falling water.

The winter solstice—December 22—when the days begin to grow longer once again, speaks to me, despite the snowy months ahead, of turning the corner toward spring.

That word "solstice" (from the Latin meaning roughly "sun standing") expresses the ancient belief that the sun actually stops still for a day before swinging us back toward itself, its warmth and light. These next two poems explore that old idea.

REVISITING SOLSTICE

Cropped grass is spiking now
above the thinning blanket of the snow,
and branches all are bare again,
their gleaming white and temporary garments
shrugged off below in crystal heaps
by last evening's late and scarcely warming sun.
The dogs, my diminutive fierce terriers,
will find it easier underfoot when I lead them—
as I soon will—on their necessary walk
just after sunrise, better say firstlight,
since the sun, in despite of yesterday's solstice,
has elected to be listed in absentia and sent along
instead a senior committee of gray clouds
to issue dark reports of snow before evening.

They used to claim the sun stood still
for a day, this time of year, then turned around
and headed back to greener, warmer climes.
But now, knowing—alas—so much more,
we realize that nothing stands still, ever.
And that those who try are doomed, nevertheless,
just like the rest of us, to whirling on
and on until we join again this spinning dust
the stars are made from, in its voyage round
the swirling curves of spiralled space and time.

Not that you'd notice,
mutters the urgent tug on
the leash held tight in either hand.

WINTER SOLSTICE

Nothing stands still,
least of all the measuring sun
for all the way, this time of year,
she seems to linger round horizons
far too long, while that river
no one ever steps into twice might be
stepped onto fairly firmly,
with some sense of permanence,
these late-Advent frigid mornings.
Nothing stands still.
And yet, between one frosted breath
and its successor, one creaking wing flap
and the next of that ancient crow
scavenging against the whitening sky,
a stopping can take place,
a holding operation, looking round
and catching breath before the next
whatever, that can save a day,
a season, year, a life from tedium,
transform it to Te Deum.

PRE-NATIVITY—DECEMBER 23

There had to be a star involved,
stars have ever had that two-edged tendency
toward portending, if given half a chance.
Last evening's light-strewn firmament,
spread wide above my own quotidian
bedtime walking with the dogs,
reminded me what day it was about to be.
"Tomorrow will be Christmas Eve Eve,"
as I informed my patient children years ago,
still do whenever I get the opportunity.

Some find the viewing of our spangled universe
leaves them lost, and at the edge of fright,
crushed beneath those swirling magnitudes.
For myself, after almost seventy Decembers
gazing upward into darkly frosted skies,
there remains a certain charged delight,
a spark that travels tight along the spine,
less apprehension than anticipation,
a persistent bright suspicion
that such far-flung loveliness bears more
than dust toward a waiting manger.

The role of "Santa's Helper" late on Christmas Eve can prove to be a challenging one.

SOME ASSEMBLY REQUIRED

Behold, one sturdy
four-year-old size frame
in day-glo, bubblegum pink
with snow white tires, grips and saddle.
With care I spread the unbagged parts
across the flattened carton
on the swept bare garage floor,
consult four languages, enigmatic diagrams,
and find myself a folding chair—
not needed thirty years ago,
the last time I assembled one of these.
Now set the front wheel bold between the forks,
and tighten wing nuts with a wrench
from the bright socket set—the extra one
her mother gave me several Christmases ago.
Next come the curving handlebars with streamers,
and the seat, white pedals too, left-handed screw
on each, so that they can't unwind and spill
my first and well-beloved granddaughter down
that steep familiar hill of scrapes and bruises.
Last the training wheels—also in white—
leaving just a glimpse of clearance either side
to support her first, tentative climb aboard
and yet provide the possibility of wings
that all too soon will soar to leave me
breathless and abandoned as she glides
glorious toward her new found flight
in laughter, life, and fleeting
splendid liberty.

This poem—another "shape poem"—reflects on the midnight Christmas Eve custom of lighting worshippers' individual candles, pew-by-pew, from the Christ candle on the Advent wreath.

THE COMING OF THE LIGHT

A
pure
and
golden
light it
seems that
spreads across
the pews reflects
its radiance from the
mellow old carved oak
and hanging greens upon
the faces, hands of those
who sing so sweetly
Silent Night. Look deep
into this gentle fire
and then go forth to bear
it far and tender to
wherever infants cold
and frightened tremble
in the dark with
no bright star
no kings
to
greet

Sermon titles have always seemed a neglected art to me. A legendary seminary professor of preaching is said to have pronounced that a title is no good "unless it can get you off the Fifth Avenue bus!" This poem grew out of a Christmas Eve sermon title of mine, "Don't Stop Me If You've Hear This One Before" that ran on our church bulletin board along Fifth Avenue.

DON'T STOP ME . . .

if you've heard this one before.
It all begins, you see,
with an amazed young virgin wondering by the well,
then proceeds, past puzzled Joseph, to a manger
in a cattle stall. Some shepherds get involved,
and three venerable Magi from the east
led by a star. A narrow escape
is followed by the usual brutalities.
And then . . .

You know the rest, of course.
But in this chill and wintered season
when depth draws near despite the merchandizing
and the malls, to hear it all once more in song,
and speech, and simple celebration,
can bring light to darkness, trust beyond all fear,
and a gentle way to walk, at least until you hear
this time-worn, secret splendid tale
for still another year.

The popular legend of "The Friendly Beasts," enjoyed nowadays by most children as an animated "Christmas Special" on TV, takes on a richer and deeper dimension in this poem.

THE SILENT SEERS

Of all the witnesses
around that holy manger
perhaps it was the animals
saw best what lay ahead
for they had paced the aching roads
slept in the wet and hungry fields
known the sharp sting of sticks
and thorns and curses
endured the constant bruise
of burdens not their own
the tendency of men to use
and then discard rather than meet
and pay the debt of gratitude.
For them the future also held
the knacker's rope, the flayer's blade
the tearing of their bodies
for the sparing of a race.
In the shadows of that stable
might it be his warmest welcome
lay within their quiet comprehending gaze?

An imaginary character, to be sure. But one who might well have been present in that "lowly cattle shed."

THE MIDWIFE OF BETHLEHEM

Why do we make such a fuss,
after all, about birth?
Surely we know what is happening,
bound to happen sooner or later,
disease, drink, cold blind accident,
too little food, too many brains,
the usual and always final event
gets them all, get us all in the end.
So why, in the name of heaven,
are all these idiot shepherds here,
far from their fold, fouling the air
and the streets with their rancid flocks?
And these dark, distinguished strangers,
confused, spent with much travel,
mumbling together of stars, gold, other gifts?
Indeed you'd think even the dumb beasts
in their stalls had been told something
and were waiting, reverent somehow
at this hasty, unprovided birth.
Yet, when all is said and done,
there was something about that young mother,
trusting, calm, confident for a first timer.
And the baby, so bold, aware already . . .
Why, I do believe the child is smiling,
looking right over here, bless my soul, at me.
Get out of my way, sheep,
while I kneel a moment, rest my weary legs
before I leave, and view this newest infant
that my red old hand has slapped
from death to free and gasping life
this odd, and almost holy night.

Today's preachers, it seems to me, tend to stress the human side of the incarnation mystery. They seem eager to emphasize the fleshly, humble, even demeaning aspects of it all. Yet might we, in so doing, risk neglecting the equally vital truth that it was Almighty God, the Lord of Hosts, Creator of the Cosmos, who actually stooped to join us at Bethlehem?

MINIMIZING MAGIC

We celebrate the ordinary in our time,
point out the muddy messiness of stables
and those friendly beasts,
accentuate the workaday of shepherds,
the astrological expertise of magi,
Mary's teenage pregnancy,
and the impact of that winter's journey
on poor Joseph's job security.
All this tells us—we are fond
of pointing out—that Christ can come
in our time as well, that our God is born
right at the heart of things just as they are
and always have been.

While all the time
a blazing star and angels,
prostrate, bedazzled shepherds,
amazing and alarming kings with gifts,
an immaculate, adoring blue-caped mother,
and an age-old, new-born God on golden straw
sing wonder to our weary ears,
shine glory to our bleary eyes,
and charm us to that old eternal realm
where everything is seen shot through
with marvel, mystery and miracle,
and the ordinary disappears,
absorbed into the holy.

A New Year trip to New Hampshire to be with a friend facing a difficult diagnosis led to this reflection alongside the frozen lake in the shadow of the White Mountains.

TOLTEC POINT—WINNIPESAUKEE
—December 31st, 1995—(For Bob)

A year's last daylight fades
along the lake. Skaters wheel
in frozen silence by the farther shore,
while the dark heave of the Ossippee—
Black Snout to Shaw—sleeps
beneath its mottled winter spread.

There is a clear-cut, necessary
quality to the closing of the calendar
in climes like these; a sense of "ages past"
and yet to be that leads the eye across
the ice's white expanse toward
the pine and fir-clad slopes
and then the lingering pink and blue
of final sunset . . . lends itself
to framing new perspectives round
these matters of mortality,
tomorrow's drive into the city's dark,
whatever waits beyond . . .
reminds the solitary inner part—
savoring a silent hour before
the party and the popping of the corks—
how much remains of loveliness and rest,
even at the heart of winter's grim necessity.

Looking back across a year, and revisiting the various holy days and seasons, I am struck by the contrast with my Calvinistic boyhood in Scotland where even Christmas was a regular working day, and Easter just another Sunday.

SEASONINGS

The gentle, sure progression
of four candled Sabbaths toward the manger,
those forty purple proving days to find a way
from winter into spring, scarlet Pentecost,
and shining bright Epiphany,
such feastings, fasts, and festivals—
the numbering and naming of the days and weeks—
played little part within the Calvinistic calendar
of my Scottish boyhood years.
"All Catholic mumbo jumbo . . . hocus pocus"
was the general grim consensus.
"Just show me, if you can,
where you find this in the Bible."

Even so does zeal,
and dry, unliberated intellect, strip life
from life, diminish holy wonder, and in the name
of barren truth alone leave days and years,
and faith itself, impoverished.

The next few poems derive from boyhood wartime experiences. I lived out most of the years of the Second World War (1939—1945) in an industrial city in the north of England where bombing was a fairly familiar experience.

BOMB FRAGMENT
   (on my study wall)

Sixty years ago and more
you fell black from the open belly
of a Heinkel or a Junkers over Yorkshire
in the siren-panicked night, slammed tight
into the crisp topped tar-macadam
of our new suburban Drive
and burned your little liquid hell of hate—
incendiary white—across the melting gravel chips
where, last week, I had skinned my knees
in falling from a bike.

Dad, the Air Raid Warden,
bore you home in an old moldy sack
to show his buried boys, deep in the backyard
air-raid shelter just what the war was all about,
while Dick—the younger one—woke up in fright
and vomited his supper in the damp and earthy dark.

Before he died Dad entrusted you to me,
"As the oldest . . ."—how he put it—
"the one who remembers." So you became an heirloom,
one of very few, along with the brass nameplate
from the door of my Scots baker granddad's house.
Until now, in a still darker, doom-divining season,
I test your heft against my praying palm,
and sense, beneath the skin, a conflagration,
once evaded, that awaits its fated—
almost final—moment to consume.

DREAMHAVEN

Even before D-Day
and the great emptying out
of England's fields and hedgerows
—one vast and camouflaged parking lot—
onto the harrowed beaches of the French,
even before those daily tidal waves of bombers
bearing east about sunset to deliver our turn,
even after the buzzbombs, doodlebugs—
names to tame them into toys they never were—
came skittering across our skies in random hate,
cigar ends glowing frightful in the dark,
Mum and Dad decided that the cold and earthy damp
of our backyard Anderson shelter posed more risk
than the odd incendiary bomb. When the warning
sounded from the factory roof they would bed us down
beneath the tough oak table round which we ate our meals,
wrote letters, diaries, drew and painted, did the homework
we brought back from school—still sandbagged from
the big one landing in the lower playground.
It was the closest Dick and I came
to a camping trip those confined cautionary years
and whatever fears still lingered lay concealed beneath
the tangled maze of bedclothes, pillows, table legs.
"Is that the all clear, Daddy" we would ask
of that second wailing siren, far later in the night,
reassured and yet reluctant, somehow,
to forsake the secret shelter of our cozy bivouac.
Then back upstairs to bed,
dread now, if not dissolved, deferred at least
until some deeper, even darker night to come.

WITH HIS STRIPES

Still just a Yorkshire lad,
my wounded Uncle Albert,
back from Germany on leave,
and no longer a sergeant, told of how,
in the field hospital, having heard of Nazi saboteurs
blowing up such places with disguised grenades,
he had launched himself from bed to tackle
an officer/surgeon hard into the mud, just as
the victim opened up his mess tin—Mills Bomb—lunch,
convinced he, and the rest of that blood-wearied ward,
were doomed to kingdom come, or thereabouts.
"The daft thing was . . ." he told us, "his odd accent
wasn't German, but, I think, some sort of Scottish."
"Opened up my bloody wound again,"
he added with a grin, "that, and this
pale and vacant space here on my sleeve."

FIRST FEAR

. . . as back as I recall,
was the coal-hole right beside
and to the left of our red-painted,
stylish-stained-glass-paneled front door.
The soot-spitting, fierce-eyed,
permanently bent-backed,
leather-hatted delivery men—
with flaps down to their shoulders
just like the French Foreign Legion
only pit black, not Sahara white—
would hump the brimming sacks
swaying bowlegged from their cart
out by the garden gate then dump them
with a knee-jerking shoulder-topping slump
and swoop so that the open end came down
astride the dark, unlidded cavity
and precious fuel went crashing,
scraping, tumbling, heaping in
onto the steady growing mound
boxed in the cellar below.

Days when Dad forgot,
or Mum had lost, the house key,
I was the one elected,
by right of the firstborn—
yet still slim and small enough
to slide that narrow slope—
selected to slip-squeeze
down through that hole into the house
to let the family in.
Slides should be fun for children
but Oh! that feet-first, blind
and grimy, groping, grip-losing,
then slipping, tipping fall
to darkness and the drop

right at the end
onto the shifting,
sinking top of a steep
unsteady pile of sharp and rattling,
rolling-off-into-the-distance chunks
of dark and dusty rock!

Then the staggering,
grasping clamber, gasping from the bin,
across the cobwebbed cellar to the stairs
and up, in spider-black night—
don't think,
hold that imagination iron-tight—
to find the light switch
or the handle to the door beneath
the hanging coats—whichever met
the panicked searching hand—
and illuminate the blessed kitchen,
bolts to the rear door now
slipping back and swinging wide
to find the family impatient there
to get inside and on with making
tea and chores and toilet trips
as I scrubbed away the stains,
wiping blank terror from my mind
into my vaulted memory and
still scrambling hope.

FALLING AWAY

These Yorkshire fells and dales
appear ever to be falling away,
toppling from Emily's wuthering heights
into wide accommodating valleys
carved by Derwent, Calder, Ribble and the rest,
then trimmed by flocks of patient sheep
that crop the slopes and shoulders round
toward that verdant jeweled Jerusalem
folk hereby love to sing about.

Up here, along the tops, however,
driving tight along the teetering edge,
mad vertigo hangs you out there in the balances,
suspended in that stomach-clutching space
between this summit and the next,
flung far into the spinning turn,
the terrible excellence of things.

Might it be that way also at the end,
nothing all that dark and dreadful,
but a life-demanding climb,
agonizing to be sure, all the gasping way
along and up some looming harsh escarpment
grasping toward the final summit where, at last,
you stumble forward into emptiness
to find everything . . . all at once?

THE NEWS SO FAR . . .

"He's dead at present."
My father, in his latest years, would say
of this or that old friend, just recently departed.
Signifying, perhaps, a taste of bitter humor,
something writers might describe
as being "said with a wry grin."
He's dead at present.
And he is too, dead now, indeed,
these eighteen years and more,
yet still granting me a momentary grin,
and just one nagging question.
Was it really all a joke? Or might
a gentle hint of promise, hope, and even faith,
be caught behind, between that witty present
of a smile he sent my way, and this one?

From time to time I have been commissioned to compose poems for special occasions. This poem was commissioned by the Wallingford Presbyterian Church to be set as an anthem for the celebration of their new organ and renovated chancel. The poem was set to music by noted composer and choral director Donald Nally.

CADENZA—A NEW SONG TO THE LORD

There is a unity in song
transcends the steep divisions of the mind,
a melting power in melody that leaps high
across all boundaries and barriers,
defies all sharp and cruel distinctions of the in
and out, the orthodox and heretic,
the saved and damned.

This mystic music that we make
makes us, then lifts us to another realm
where time and space suspend,
duty dissolves, fear disappears,
and even self itself grows thin,
is lost and found again resounding
in the crystal sounding of the spheres.

Whatever lies ahead—this heaven we hope for—
here and now, within these years
we catch, are blessed to see at least a glimpse
of what is yet to be in all these gifted moments
when, with voices, instruments,
"psalms, hymns, and spiritual songs"
We can set free our captive souls
to join God's age-old oratorio,
soaring in momentary majesty.

STAINED GLASS WINDOWS

They have a way of turning
light to song transforming rays
of radiant sun to sounds that resonate
with rich and wondrous harmonies, Gregorians,
plainsongs, yes, Charles Wesley too and Isaac
Watts, so that the pews and even people are
caught up into, submerged in, washed over
by, a rainbow palette that spells grace
sings God in every chord and color of
this bright creation in the meantime
telling stories, showing heroes, helping
incidents—long dusted into history—
know life again, wear faces, catch and lift
the bright imagination toward height so that
two faces—voices become one, communion takes
on living flesh, and faith finds strength
within the past to move into the future
wearing sunlight unafraid.

This poem was commissioned by members of the Swarthmore Presbyterian Church as a gift for their son and daughter-in-law who were moving to a new home in a new town, a new state.

HOUSEWARMING
—For Alan and Lynne Dugan

A home is beyond geography
defies precise location on these maps
we are so eager to create as if they
really told us where we are.
Home is a construct of the heart
and soul, begins the very day
that we are "taken home"—
a tiny refugee—from hospital
in cardboard box or bassinette.
Its secret places are developed
through the childhood years
in times of quiet solitude and prayer.
Its hearth, where lives are joined,
games played and stories told
is always somewhere near the center.
While the dinner table, yes, the entire kitchen
resonates with sacramental meals and moments,
all the holiness that hides in daily things.

We are, in fact, like snails,
and carry our homes with us, setting them down
from place to place, adding at times a room,
a person here and there to share it with us.
Despite the unreal estate people no one
ever sold, will ever sell a home.
The most they can provide is roof and walls,
a threshold to step over.
The rest, thank God, is up to us,
and up to Him who set this longing
deep within, until our final coming home.

Many churches publish cookbooks, compiled by their members, both as a fundraising method, and also to foster fellowship. Some of my wife's most valued recipes have come from such efforts. This poem was commissioned for the preface to such a book.

RECIPE—FOR A CHURCH COOKBOOK

Nourishment must be more
than merely fuel for running on,
fodder for the furnace that consumes
our hours in furious haste.
There is an art to eating, old
as breaking of a loaf, the sharing
of a deep, refreshing cup. Each meal,
if touched with light imagination,
a modicum of care,
can lead to miracles of more
than multiplying fish and bread,
transforming water into wine,
can bring about the forming and re-forming
of that sacred circle shaped in trust
and sealed by eyes and hands across a table
where the grace, once said,
is then revealed in every morsel,
fragment, sip or swallow savored
in the feast that feeds and heals our days.

Old chiming clocks have long fascinated me. We have five of them, at last count, in our home. The clock in the poem below stood in my study at the church and its regular tick-tock, and its melodious chimes, spoke to me each Sunday of the dimensions of my call to preach the gospel.

CLOCK MINDER

I wind it every Sabbath
before preaching, retrieve
the tarnished old brass key
from between its battered oaken feet,
flip open the glass face then turn
and turn the ratchet right,
recharging the tight coil to chart
the falling springs and springing falls
that score the twining seasons—
two sockets for two windings,
first the hands, then the chimes—
just as I climb the six steep steps
to launching off upon the most time-clad
yet time-defeating task ever was entrusted
to one formed of clay and spirit breath.
My calling too to tell—or toll—the hours,
remind how many and how few, evoke a looking
backward to review before the leap ahead,
but also to resound, to echo forth a resonance
beneath and all around the measuring moments,
shape word and sound about a timelessness
that sings and soars the sonorous deeps
beyond the numbering of days.

Balancing the call to preach is the call to be a pastor, to be present with your people at times of great joy and great sorrow. It is a most challenging, arduous and sensitive role to fill. It is a privilege to be called to fill it.

CALLING

Both less and more than family and good friends,
still you belong there at the high moments and low,
included in the laughter and the tears, all the embraces,
gestures of delight and consolation across the years,
even participating in remembering, noting the absences,
the gaps among the circled chairs, the ones
who couldn't make it for whatever reason, glad or sad.

Yet for all the long and hard-earned familiarities,
you are also set apart. You have a role to play, a place to fill,
a dimension toward which it is your duty and your privilege
to focus everyone's attention. Your task to speak the words
and open up the silences that unite, lend shape and texture,
and at least a glimpse of the beyond within these
joyful/painful moments crammed with here and now.

If you can do it, if you can evoke and hold together
both this world and the next, if you can somehow embody,
even for the instant of a handclasp or a prayer,
that sheer intensity of presence that fills all absence
with new hope, then they may realize they have a pastor,
then you may even touch the fringes of the garment of the Master.

That which makes it all possible.

ERODING

Prayer rips me out from the rock layer of self,
wears me in through the shore-strand skin
of this fractured creation, wades me
through every you and me gathered
like sand to be washed far and
wide with the reach and the
rush of the full-moon and
earth-brimming tide
to the deep of
an ocean
called
God.

REASONS

But that's just wishful thinking,
she objected, never noticing, I guess,
that in her stern resolve to face
all of those stubborn facts,
she was indulging a desire no less
insistent than my own.

Surely everything we think is born within—
still bears—a wish or two,
if nothing else the wish to make some sense
out of this running stumble of scenarios,
events and individuals.
Perhaps the best that we can ever think
is crammed with wishes,
and whatever truth we touch lies rooted
deep in everlasting wanting,
in this altogether human need
to move beyond what is,
toward what might be.

WHY I STILL GO

For all their quirks and quibbles, all their foibles,
squabbles, even downright donnybrooks,
I find my people there.
Recalcitrant, to be sure, concerning this issue,
or that. As reluctant as those first followers
to accept what fairest Jesus brought to life.

Yet singing the same sweet songs,
murmuring familiar prayers.
admitting, as I must, that another week
has worn its way, no closer to the kingdom,
hungering, across years of disappointment,
for words that ring so clear they melt
the frozen marrow, drag you back again—
despite—to trust, compassion, even resolution.

For all my weary, reasoned doubt,
the continuing disillusion and despair
of this already blood-drenched century,
for all my anger at her blind echoing
of the worst that hides in all of us,
come Sunday morning, somehow,
I still find myself in church.

I am more and more convinced that Jesus' message was not so much about sin and repentance—that was John the Baptist's job—but was about seeing properly; about discerning the presence, power and grace of God in and through every aspect of existence. That was what his parables were all about, disclosing the kingdom of God in everyday objects and events. That is what he meant when he proclaimed, "The kingdom of God is at hand." "At hand" means within reach, right at your fingertips. This poem, and the ones that follow, seek to illustrate that understanding.

SIGNIFICANT

You literally make a sign—
at least that's what your Latin signifies—
pick up a magic marker and insert,
inscribe yourself below the cheerful face,
"Hello, my name is . . ."
tack or staple a blank piece of cardboard
right across a slat of lumber scrap
and scrawl upon it what it is you have to say,
whatever it is you love, or hate, or even live for.
"Notice Me!" you call out,
"Pay Attention—Over Here!"

But now supposing, for a moment,
that every single thing might be significant,
and all creation, like those malling throngs
in Washington DC massed there
before Abe Lincoln's chair,
is demonstrating, for God's sake, and ours too,
is waving, hailing, placarding to us,
and giving notice, "Here I am now. Heads Up.
Over Here. Stop, Look, and Listen."
There just may be more to this—
don't you see?—than meets the eye.

SEEING WHOLE

What if Columbus,
despite his crimes, was
right after all and this world
had no edges for sailing over
tumbling to the bottomless dark?
Suppose all borders were beginnings
as well as endings and no one knew
just where so that, like Monet's
Water Lilies, you didn't need your eyes
half-closed to see that beauty has no
boundaries, that there's no end of
things to see, and you and I
are part, parcel too, of those
black holes/white springs where
worlds emerge new born into
the smiling light.

SECRET

The truth, or so he came
to tell us, will not be caught
and held within the ordered paragraphs
and pages of a treatise or elaborated dogma,
does not lend itself to concise delineation
or precise and tidily presented definition,
is never to be found locked tight inside
those capsulated catchword phrases,
slogans, live-or-die-for credos that we love
to force down one another's throats.
Rather is to be glimpsed across a table,
fireside, subway car, or early morning meadow,
a late lingering fragrance, echo of tears
or laughter, a child's response to
this world's daily mystery, a gift revealed
in every moment we can look and listen
to each other, see, and sing that living truth
that woos us, weds us, weaves us in
and through the holy fabric of our days.

FOUNTAIN—BROOKLYN BOTANICAL GARDEN

It was your basic fountain really,
nothing elaborate,
no nonsense of cavorting nymphs
or horses prancing
beneath sporting sea gods,
dolphins spouting
among the tumbling waters.
A simple saucer stone and base,
wedge and dish, no more, elegant
sufficiency for dancing, fitting
place from which to soar through liquid
winging space to a toppling downpour,
splashing light into the glancing pool below.
And then to flow,
and mount again, mimicking
the circling rain of this bright chancing
fountain world, source of every springing
flight and fall.

Music has long been a source of inspiration for me. My father was a fine trumpet player and since the age of eight I have also been a brass musician. In making, and listening to fine music I suspect we come as close to heaven as we are permitted to in this life.

ON HEARING BRUCKNER'S NINTH AGAIN

There is no end to this. He tried.
God knows that pious old Austrian tried,
spending half of his remaining days in prayer
pleading time enough to set it down,
to gather up his notes and then compose
a final movement that would pull it all together,
all those crashing chords and deafening pauses,
the sad sepulchral scherzo
with its naked tendon-plucking pizzicati,
and those eerie plangent melodies emerging
almost fully formed, then vanishing just before
they grasped toward fulfilment, or conclusion.

He was still writing as he died,
still building up his towering walls of sound—
sonorities born in his beloved organ loft—
balancing chord on top of chord until
they crashed and toppled over
to shrill silence once again,
still ringing out with every ounce and instant left
that every living moment echoes,
sounding and resounding, to set up
such resonances as will never be resolved
but reverberate across and down, defying all finales
in the endless singing of the spheres.

A traveling exhibit on "The Silk Road" displayed, among many other fascinating items, several sets of mummified remains. One such "mummy," the richly dressed and remarkably well preserved body of a young woman, was described as "The Beauty of Xiaohe."

THE BEAUTY OF XIAOHE

*(On viewing her mummified remains at
the University of Pennsylvania Museum)*

So that's where your Silk Road
was leading to, past Petra
and its towering, cliff-cut Treasury,
across all those carved out camel trails, oases,
caravanserais, the loess fields of Samarkand,
and Central Asia's steppes, and finally
that dry and desiccating desert where
your mortal flesh took on
this strange form of immortality.
The acid salts and frigid winter played
their preserving part, and now you lie,
well-wrapped, but somehow radiant,
coiled in your linen covers, goat-skin boots,
and jaunty, feathered hat, a hat that failed—
thanks be!—to hold your rich, brown hair
from spilling steep and wide beneath your shoulders.
I gaze across almost four thousand years
of wandering, wondering who, and why,
and if you could have been as lovely
as your high cheek bones, full lips,
and tightly banded chin suggest,
seeking at least a spark of recognition
from beneath those full, luxuriant lashes,
glimpsing, at last, and holding to
the fierce hope that clothed you thus,
set precious food and drink—a traveler's
eucharist—viaticum—there by your side,
then sent you forth to destinations
far beyond my present time and place.

I retired from the First Presbyterian Church in the City of New York in the spring of 2000. Eighteen months later, on September 11, 2001, I was summering in Maine when the twin towers of the World Trade Center were destroyed. Eight people from my former congregation, along with other friends and acquaintances, were killed in that terrible event. During the following weeks and months I traveled to New York to counsel with friends and to assist at funerals. The following poems reflect on those days of grief and loss.

AMENDED CREDO

They miss it out at the island church
I worship in for the summer months.
Standing each week to recite the creed
then catching me flat-footed,
right after ". . . crucified, dead and buried."
with no ". . . descended into hell."
They just press right on for heaven
without even a backward glance,
while I—incurably Presbyterian—
slip it in anyway, then hurry to catch up.

Never missed it all that much
until last month, the Sunday after
the twin towers fell, and we saw hell
spread fiery across our screens.
"He descended into Hell," I said out loud,
because that's precisely where he was
five days before, comforting his children,
cradling them in his arms, his deep pierced hands,
and bearing them back home with him
to share his place at God's right hand.

On the car radio while driving to New York City for a funeral that September I heard a commentator describing some of the 9/11 memorial services in the most scathing terms. Later that day, visiting historic Saint Paul's Chapel, miraculously preserved right on the edge of the abyss, those jarring words contrasted sharply with all that I saw taking place there.

A VISIT TO SAINT PAUL'S CHAPEL

PORT-A-JOHNS—some thirty of them—
line the foot of the church steps,
facing outward onto Broadway.
The elegant pillared portico is become
a gratis cafeteria; hot soup, sandwiches, soda,
all kinds of fruit, cakes and candy,
with chairs and tables set in sunlight
and rescue workers, soldiers, police officers
and volunteers relaxing and eating together.
Almost a holiday scene, except for the dust,
the heavy, clinging smell of burning,
and the absence of laughter.

Inside, the historic pews are furnished
with blankets, quilts and pillows
while the side aisles overflow with toiletries.
A grand piano stands smothered in stuffed animal toys.
The entire sacred space festooned with banners:
      TO NEW YORK AND ALL ITS RESCUERS
      KEEP YOUR SPIRITS UP
      OKLAHOMA LOVES YOU!!
hangs from a balcony, while on a pillar:
      YOU RAN IN WHEN
      WE ALL RAN OUT.
      FOR THAT WE ARE FOREVER GRATEFUL.
      GOD BLESS BM LADDER 20.

A letter in the pew rack from a choirgirl in Tucson says:
>   I wanted you to know that you had a friend
>   in Tucson who was praying for you.
MASSAGE THERAPY reads a sign in one corner,
CHIROPRACTORS occupy another.
The proud George Washington pew is filled
with podiatrists under FOOT CARE. Along the rear,
on the very brink of hell, stretches a rack of solid work boots.
"The wreckage and intense heat shred the workers' footgear."
said my volunteer escort/guide from Asheville, NC.
A noontime prayer service begins.
"The self-satisfied bromides of organized religion,"
as one sophisticated critic said recently on NPR.
Twenty or so unsophisticated rescue workers,
National Guard troops, and peace officers
stand to pray and listen for Good News,
still others simply sleep.
<u>et lux in tenebris lucet</u>—
and the darkness has not overcome it.

MAIL FROM NEW YORK CITY

He wrote that he was walking,
late to work, south on Seventh Ave,
and was startled by a huge plane
flying low overhead and obviously lost.
He watched as it flew in,
counted down the floors to where
the flames began on level ninety-eight,
the floor on which his wife,
mother of the children
he had just dropped off at school,
was already hard at work.
Then began running.

She wrote that, as head chef
at the Gay Men's Health Center in the Village,
she grabbed the van, plus a couple of helpers,
overloaded it with food—
leftover BBQ chicken and lollipops—
and headed downtown, picking up
a police escort, no less,
on the way to ground zero,
passing out sandwiches and water
at every roadblock, and then serving
twenty pieces of blessedly still hot chicken
to stunned and dusty heroes from the NYPD.

She described how,
From her rooftop,
They watched the towers burning.
And as the first one fell,
Her weeping friends stretched out
their hands as if to try
to hold it still in place, as if
to keep their world
from crumpling to dust.

SETTING UP THE ADVENT WREATH—NOVEMBER 2001

This wooden wheel that perches
on the six-foot, stout oak post
seems to demand more thought this time,
more careful, patient balancing
than it has seen in years gone by . . .
something about the way things tumble down,
the tendency of structures to collapse upon themselves
and spill tomorrow's bright anticipation
across the old, unyielding earth.

These fragile points of fire,
alighting, in progression,
on four purple and pink candles
betray a silent trembling that reveals
far more than any simple unseen motion of the air.
While their waxing light across December's weeks
discloses utter darkness once again,
an ancient void, upon whose brink
this wounded year bends, teetering between
the birth of hope and new awakened terror.

HOMELAND SECURITY—THE EVE OF ADVENT

Times like these—
what with daily news of terror,
the random ways of cold malevolence,
fanatic dedication to the cause of death—
the usual comforts of this season
can seem thin, at best,
and threadbare,
offering scant protection
from December's dying days.

Times like these
may yet recall a child,
whose birth was framed by bloodshed
and a bleak indifference,
who found seeming scant protection
in a mother's arms, a father's watchful wisdom,
that old, eternal tenderness, whose shield
is still the only, sure, and best defense
against the savage dark.

POST EPIPHANY—JANUARY 2002

Looking back, before we turn
to face the numbing coldness up ahead,
it seemed, somehow, a simpler,
much more elemental season this time around.
We had not known that dark could be so deep,
so visible, so almost tangible.
So that the light, when it came—
less brilliant, to be sure—
pierced sharper, further in, closer to the core,
revealing, after long, luxurious absence,
that hint—no more, but then, no less—
that least, yet strangely lasting sign
of birth in great privation.
With this sufficient blessing for our times
we can, at least, set out again.

Finally two poems to sum up what I have glimpsed and tried to put into words between mirage and miracle.

WORLDLY WISDOM?

I'm still looking, scanning,
skipping right to the end at times,
or settling for the gist on the first page,
reading—more selectively across the years—
but reading just the same, in the news
and novels, articles and extracts, poems even . . .
searching for the one, the word, the sentence
that can tell me what it's all about,
why I'm here, will not be here much longer,
where this morning's golden-leaving
autumn beauty comes from,
why, and what it's for,
who thought this whole thing called existence up
and maybe has a clue about its shape
and size and possible duration.
While all the time, beneath, behind,
beyond the endless pages,
the unrelenting streaming of the words,
it unquestionably happens,
keeps on happening,
without any hope or need for explanation,
moving on, while I stand wordless,
gasping in its tumbling wake.

LAY OF THE LAND

Evil and good endure;
the rest is history,
it's endless ebb and flow,
the daily onset of events
and circumstances.

We arrive and pass away
and, in between—
that curt, fragmented meantime—
taste cruelty, experienced or
passed along, the slow
and angry bitterness
of absence, injury and loss,
with every now and then
a momentary exaltation;
generosity perhaps,
uniting's glimpse of ecstasy,
and the fidelity of longing.

In the end it all begins
again and whichever wins or loses
never is announced.
Kindness, however, does appear
to wear exceeding well,
while laughter shapes a bright,
persistent music.

www.ingramcontent.com/pod-product-compliance
Lightning Source LLC
Chambersburg PA
CBHW071334190426
43193CB00041B/1799